Modesty Matters

Expanded and Revised Edition

Susan M. Watson
(Formerly Susan M. Hataway)

Modesty Matters

Copyright © 2025
Susan M. Watson

ALL Rights Reserved

No portion of this publication may be reproduced, stored in any electronic system, or transmitted in any form or by any means, electronic, mechanical, photocopy, recording, or otherwise, without written permission from the author. Brief quotations may be used in literary reviews.

All scripture quotations are taken from the King James Version of the Holy Bible.

ISBN: 978-0-9746661-2-9

For information or for speaking appointment contact:

apostolicrosepublishing@gmail.com
or
swatsonauthor@gmail.com

To all faithful Christian ladies, your faith and grace are true examples. Your strength of character is an uplifting inspiration...

Contents

1. Sharper Than a Two-Edged Sword
2. The Guidance of Our Mind
3. Being Meek
4. Only The Humble
5. True Love Conquers
6. As He Forgives
7. Necessity Of Faith
8. Dedication To Prayer and Worship
9. True Holiness
10. Our Outer Appearance

Acknowledgments

First and foremost, I want to thank my Lord and Savior, Jesus Christ. Without you I am nothing. I would also like to express my heartfelt gratitude to my husband who has supported and encouraged me throughout the process of writing this book. Your unwavering belief in my vision and your constant prayers have been an invaluable source of strength. I am especially thankful for the dedicated Christian ladies whose lives have inspired these pages, and for the friends and family who have uplifted me with their words of encouragement and acts of kindness. This book would not have been possible without your support, guidance, and love. Thank you for walking this journey with me.

Chapter 1
Sharper Than a Two-Edged Sword

I thought I would discuss the tongue first because it's the main thing that gets us in trouble and the hardest thing to control. The tongue is a fire not easily quenched. We can burn someone's reputation with just a word or sentence. We must watch the tongue constantly because it will blurt out things we don't intend to say. Once something is said it cannot be taken back. You can say, *oh I didn't mean to say that* all you want, but it's too late to take it back. It has already been said, it's out there for anyone around to hear. People will look at you and listen to you and think, *I'm not sure I want what she has.* They will assume if you're that loose with your tongue then you probably aren't living what you say in other ways. Or that you will talk about them behind their back also. That's not good, that's not what we want. We want others to hear us talk and want what we have. We don't want them to hear us put others down. They don't want to hear that. Nobody wants to hear backbiting and complaining. They want to hear us lifting others up and praising God! The old saying *if you don't have anything nice to say don't say anything at all,* is a wonderful saying. We've heard that phrase since we were young. But do we obey it? If we all took heed to it, we wouldn't get in as much trouble. We must remember it's not what goes into the mouth that defiles, it's what comes out. What we speak!

Matthew 15:11 says it so well, Not that which goeth into the mouth defileth a man; but that which cometh out of the mouth, this defileth a man. That scripture says it plainly. Defile means to make foul; to pollute. Our tongue can pollute us. It can contaminate our heart and make us stink from the inside out. And don't worry, anyone that gets near us will smell the stench. They will hear the backbiting and want to get as far away from us as possible. And I don't blame them! Let's be honest ladies, how would we feel if we heard someone constantly talking about others. And if we really think about it, we've all known at least one person just like that. That's definitely not what Christian ladies do. Instead, let's love one another and keep the things we may know about each other in our hearts. May we disclose them only to the Lord in prayer.

If we love life and want to see good days, we must learn to clamp our tongue and refrain from speaking evil. When the Lord saves us, we can't continue to talk as we used to. We no longer bicker and complain about everything. We definitely don't tell tales or someone else's secrets that they trust us with. We are to lead quiet and peaceful lives. We are to seek peace and ensue it. *1Timothy 2: 2-3* says, *...that we may lead a quiet* *and peaceable life in all godliness and honesty. For this is good and acceptable in the sight of God our Savior.* I know sometimes we have a habit of wanting to talk too much. Especially when we get around our friends. I don't know what it is about this generation that believes they must follow the crowd. It's like they feel they can't have their own thoughts and beliefs. We can't look toward the false witnesses of this world as examples, but we need to keep our eyes and thoughts on Jesus. He is the true example of purity and modesty. We must stand up for what is right and good. I know peer pressure is real and it's difficult. I know it's hard sometimes to not join the group. But being different isn't a bad thing and neither is standing up for what we believe in. We are Christian ladies, we don't get intimidated, and we have no desire to follow the worldly crowd. We want to walk that straight and narrow path that leads to life not the wide path that leads to destruction. *Matthew 7:13* states, *Enter ye in at the straight gate: for wide is the gate, and broad is the way, that leadeth to destruction...*

We must be very careful what we say because when we loosely talk, things tend to slip out in our conversations that we later regret. Let's not tell or talk about others' secrets or sins (or make up any either). Let's show love, God's love, that others will see our actions, hear our conversations and want what we have. Let's bring them to the Lord with our pure conversations, and our true repentant hearts. *Put away from thee a froward mouth, and perverse lips put far from thee, Proverbs 4:24.* Our actions and words are very powerful. They can make someone having a good day have a bad one. We can't say something and take it back, it's not possible, we've already spoken it. The action is already there. We can't take it back. And whoever is around already heard it. We can say we don't gossip and talk badly about people all we want, but if someone else hears us doing just that, then they won't believe a word we say.

We must be the example of goodness, of purity

and not of evil speaking. To be modest we must put perverseness far from us. We cannot be wolves in sheep's clothing. We can't pretend to love others to their face and talk badly about them when their backs are turned. The Bible doesn't say to put perverse lips a short distance from you (just until their back is turned). It says rather, put them *far* from you. By our words we will be justified or condemned. It is either one way or the other. Either we are kind to others and help them with the kind words we say, or we will be condemned for our maliciousness. The mean, unthoughtful words we say that hurt others. We must constantly watch what we say. When we speak or converse with people, we're to use wisdom. We should never just spit out words without first stopping and thinking about what we are going to say. If what we want to say is spiteful and mean, it's best to hold our tongue and not say anything. If we can't speak with love, kindness and compassion we're better off keeping our thoughts to ourselves. *But I say unto you, that every idle word that men shall speak, they shall give account thereof in the day of judgment, Matthew 12:36.*

We will have to answer for every word we say. That makes me want to say nice things. Think of all the words we will utter in a lifetime, and every one we will have to give account for. I'd rather do right and speak right all the time than to have to worry about unrepented words I've said that I don't remember. Every word we speak, whether good or bad, we will have to give an account for on the day of judgement. Oh my, that means we must watch every word that we say, because God is listening. And even if we tell the person we are talking to not to repeat what we say, someone besides the person we are talking to has already heard the entire conversation. God heard everything we said. He's keeping a record. That's enough reason for me to hold my tongue and to say only nice things. I know it's hard, believe me I do, especially when someone has hurt us. I know it's hard not to want revenge and to hurt them back. But we can't feel that way, because what all that bitterness does to your heart isn't worth it, trust me, it will hurt you more. We must hold our tongues and pray for that person. We must forgive them for anything and everything they have done to us. And truly forgive them from our heart. Give them to God and be kind to them. Who knows, maybe by our kindness they may change their evil ways.

Even though it may seem that people don't see what is right, you never know what difference your actions and speech make on the inside. Many times, a person can be hard on the outside and act as though they don't want to hear your testimony. But you never know what God is working in the heart of that person. The outside is just a shell and sometimes it seems hard, and you feel you are unable to get through. Just keep being that example and let God do the rest. Stand strong on what is right and remember we are followers of Jesus, and examples to the world. With enough prayer and persistence their shell of pride may crack! And they could end up being wonderful witnesses for Jesus! Just be there with love when they come to you with questions. And help lead them to the right path. Remember, if we find that doing right makes us uncomfortable around our friends or others, then it might be time to think about finding new ones. We don't need a lot of wrong friends just one good right one.

And now, speaking of friends, there are those people that wonder why no one wants anything to do with them. Why no one calls or comes to visit them. Why they don't have any true friends. First, we must be a friend to have friends. Second, maybe it's because they wander from house to house being busy bodies, telling others' secrets. Maybe being conniving and malicious. Talking about what Miss so and so wore last Sunday and maybe even what the pastor preached that they didn't agree with (though it's just what they needed). Ladies, that is not Christian. It seems some people think that the sermons they need are for someone else. We should never think like that. If you are in a sermon listening to the pastor preach, then that sermon is for you. We all need to hear the preaching of God's word. A lot of times after church service is over you can hear them saying, *sister such and such should have been here to hear that message! It would have done her a world of good.* That is not what we're to be thinking or saying! God doesn't want us to feel like that. We should feel compassion and if a friend is struggling, we should pray for them and keep it between God and our self. Isn't that what a true friend and true Christian does?

Now that we've brought up being a true Christian, let's talk about that some. Are we doing what God has called us to do? Or have we learned to be idle? Have we been doing what 1 Timothy speaks of?

And withal they learn to be idle, wandering about from house to house; and not only idle, but tattlers also and busybodies, speaking things which they ought not, 1 Timothy 5:13

Have we sat on a pew for so long and for so many years that our ears have gotten dull of hearing? Do wrong things seem right? Have we put other books in front of, or in place of, our Bible? Are we sitting on a church pew because we want to be seen? Are we praying so we can say we did, to ease our conscience. Have we given our heart and speech to Jesus? Have we truly repented and given our life to Jesus by following his example? If not, now is the time to truly repent. Now is the time to tell God that we want to be right with him and not only tell him but show him also. We want to watch what we say and speak things that are right and good in the sight of Jesus. Not just for appearances sake, but because we truly want to be right with him. And we want to be true examples of a modest, Christian lady. There is no better time. Come on ladies, let's get on our knees and talk to Jesus. He loves us and understands. Trust me, he's there waiting to hear from you.

Blessed is he that readeth, and they that hear the words of this prophecy, and keep those things which are written therein: for the time is at hand.

Revelation 1:3

Chapter 2

The Guidance of Our Mind

Our thoughts can make us or break us! What we think has a great deal to do with what we do. Our thoughts can determine our mood or if we have a good or bad day. They can determine if we're nervous and full of anxiety or if we're calm. Your mind can work for you or against you. All depending on what you put in it or think on. Yes, it all comes down to what you put in your mind.

Are we speaking positive thoughts or are we letting everything get us down and speaking negatively. Everything we speak and hear is processed and stored in our mind. I know it may seem weird, but it is a fact. We must always watch what we let our mind dwell on. *For as he thinketh in his heart, so is he… Proverbs 23:7.*

That is a very powerful scripture. Really stop and think about it for a minute. What is that scripture saying? We are what we think in our heart. The saying, *speak positively and good things happen or think happy thoughts and you'll be happy.* It's all true! And it was just proven by scripture. We must be careful what we think and how long we dwell on a thought. Our thoughts can decide a lot of things for us. For instance, our thoughts can decide our mood and what we do. Everything you do or say starts with a thought. I know that's deep, but it is true. Think about it. See? I told you. We must not meditate on a bad thought. The enemy (satan) loves to work in our mind. He will torment us and put things in our mind that we would normally not think. Have you ever had a thought and asked yourself, *where did that thought come from*? Many times, it came from satan himself. He tries to sneak thoughts into your mind and if you dwell long enough and hard enough on them, he can get you to believe things that aren't true. We must push the bad thoughts away and think of good things. He's very sly and sneaky, you can be thinking something without really realizing it. Then when you do finally realize it, you're confused as to why you were even thinking it to begin with. That's because it wasn't your normal thought process. We can't help what we think, but we can help what we do with it once we think it. When a bad thought comes to our mind, we should instantly push it aside and think of a good thought. It doesn't matter what good thought you think as long as it's a good thought. It's a battleground between the forces of good and evil. But thank the Lord we know who the winner is! Jesus has already one! Yes, satan is going to try to mess with us. Yes, he's going to make us think things we shouldn't. But we can push him and his bad thoughts away by thinking on God and his word. By thinking about something good and not bad. *Beloved think it not strange concerning the fiery trial which is to try you, as though some strange thing happened unto you, I Peter 4:2.*

Don't worry, it's not just you. Bad thoughts come to everybody; no, you're not crazy! It's spiritual warfare! We must make the choice not to dwell on bad thoughts. Yes, it is a choice. A choice of who we are going to serve. It is a trial that we all go through. Is it easy? No, it's not. It's hard for everyone. If it was easy, it wouldn't be a trial. Trials have always been hard and always will be. But with God we can get through them victorious! The Lord will help us if we ask him to. We must go to the Lord in prayer and bring everything to him and before his throne. He hears us and knows every word we speak and think. He's omni present! Remember the war is won. Jesus is the winner! He's already won the war for anything that satan throws at us. And believe me he will throw every dart he can, but with God he will never hit the bullseye. It's a game he will lose. We must push the bad thoughts away and think of good things. When satan tries to throw a negative thought at me I start worshipping and praising Jesus! I concentrate on all the blessings and wonderful thing Jesus has done for me. And remember he's the winner and savior of my soul. With Jesus we can put satan under our feet and know that with him, satan nor his wicked demons can touch us. What is in you is stronger than anything satan fires your way! Catch his lies and throw them right back at him! You don't have to accept his lies! He's the number one deceiver, and you don't have to accept anything from him as truth. Because as we know no truth is in him. .... *He was a murderer from the beginning, and abode not in the truth, because there is no truth in him. When he speaketh a lie, he speaketh of his own: for he is a liar, and the father of it, John 8:44.* The Bible plainly speaks of satan being a liar and ladies he always will be. So pay no attention to him. His lies aren't worth the time it takes to listen to them.

God knows all things, and nothing can be

hidden from him. He knows everything. He knows when we think evil of someone even if we are smiling on the outside. We might be able to fool people some of the time, but we can't fool God any of the time. *I know thou canst do everything, and that no thought can be withholden from thee, Job 42:2.* We must bring every thought into captivity, and think of pure, holy things. Casting down every wicked imagination. And putting lucifer in his place, under your feet! Rebuke him. Bind him and his evil ways and thoughts and loose good thoughts. The more you practice fighting him and his thoughts the easier it will become. You just must recognize that it's from satan and push it aside. And instantly think on good things. Quote scripture, praise and worship Jesus. And always remember that he that is in you is greater than he that is in the world.

He (satan) will try to make you think higher of yourself than you ought to. *For if a man think himself to be something, when he is nothing, he deceiveth himself.* We are all nothing without God. Don't fall for satan's tricks! Be wise to his deceits. He will slither his way into your mind if you let him. Give him an inch and he will take a mile, or more. Stand strong on the word of God. Know satan for the liar that he is!

Many times, we judge others in our mind without saying a word. A lot of times our actions show we've judged in our thoughts and people can usually tell a phony smile and insincere kindness. I can tell what someone is thinking a lot of times just by the smirky expression on their face. We're not supposed to be that way. What about love and kindness. That's what the Bible teaches. If we see someone fall, we should stretch out a hand of love and help them up. Any of us could fall. We're not any better than anyone else. It doesn't matter how much money we have, or even what job we have. We could still fall just like the person that is being made fun of and being snickered at. We need to remember next time we want to judge another that it could be us just as easily, if it wasn't for the mercy and grace of God. We'd all be lost if it wasn't for Jesus. We must remember that he died for everyone's sins, not just ours. We want to bring them to Jesus not have them run in the other direction. Please ladies, we must show them love and compassion. People can tell a real Christian from a fake one. We don't want to misguide people; we want them to see true Christians and true modest ladies. Isn't that what it's all about? Bringing souls to Jesus? People that are looking for a real gem do not want a fake. They want the real thing, and they can usually tell whether we're real or not. And that means we must stay prayed up and close to Jesus. There is no good in us except through him. And we must always think before we speak. The tongue is an extension of our mind, it says what the mind thinks. So please, remember to think good, pure thoughts. We don't want to hurt others by what we say.

Let's not deceive ourselves, or anyone else either. God is what makes us good, and we'll never be perfect on this earth because of the flesh. None of us can be good in ourselves, only through the Lord and his word. Only God can save us. He died for our sins. Only he can make us clean and whole. If it feels like something is missing in your life. That there is a hole or void in your life. Let God fill it. Go to the Lord in prayer and give it all to him, he's what we need. He can take all those bad thoughts and change them for good ones. He wants to free you from every strong hold satan has on your mind. Jesus doesn't want us bound, he wants us free! He will fill that emptiness with his love and forgiveness. Only he can make us clean and whole. All glory belongs to him. It is rightfully his.

Remember, be careful what you allow your imagination to dwell on, satan can be sneaky and conniving. Cast down every thought that is against God and his word. Ask the Lord to filter what goes into your mind. He is so good. He loves us and doesn't want our mind bound by satan, he wants to break those chains that lucifer has tried to bind us with. He just wants us to ask him. Let's take some time now to pray and ask him sincerely from our hearts to heal our minds and to purify our thoughts according to his word. Go ahead, talk to him and let those bonds break free!

Finally, brethren, whatsoever things are true, whatsoever things are honest, whatsoever things are just, whatsoever things are pure, whatsoever things are lovely, whatsoever things are of good report; if there be any virtue, and if there be any praise, think on these things.

Philippians 4:8

Chapter 3
Being Meek

First, I want to start this chapter by saying that meekness is not a sign of weakness. What a lot of people don't realize is that it takes a strong person to be meek in the world we live in today. Most people are about themselves and don't care about anyone else or their feelings. Meekness is the total opposite. Meekness is truly a wonderful trait to have and it's biblical. God wants his people to be meek. Meekness is submission to God's will. The Bible even tells us to be meek as Jesus was meek. *Take my yoke upon you and learn of me; for I am meek and lowly in heart: and ye shall find rest unto your souls, Matthew 11:29.* Think about that verse for a moment. First, it says to learn of him. Jesus was meek and everything he did was with love and meekness. The more we read the word of God the more we see that his heart was for other people and not for himself. Then, as we read further, we see that it also says that we will find rest unto our souls. We sure can use rest in this busy life that we lead in the modern world. Jesus can take all that stress and anxiety from us.

Jesus is the perfect example of meekness and he shows meekness definitely isn't weakness. Jesus is far from weak. He's the perfect example of how we can be strong and meek at the same time. Meekness is a trait I want more of. I can never have enough love or meekness. Meekness shows our love for God and our desire to follow him. We must have a desire to want to be more like Jesus and his example. Throughout the Bible a picture is drawn of God's meekness. If we read the lines of his teachings and life in the Bible, we can see that no matter what he went through or what others did to him he still showed them love and meekness. It takes a strong person to be able to do that. But that's how we are supposed to be also. He even asked God to forgive them for they know not what they do. Now that's true love! So don't ever feel that God doesn't love you because he does. He loves everyone and wants all to find salvation and repentance. He will teach us meekness and show us how to be more like him if we will just be willing to let him guide us. *The meek will he guide in judgment; and the meek will he teach his way, Psalm 25:9.*

The Lord takes pleasure in his people. He loves us and loves to spend time with us. He loves to hear us pray and talk to him. He wants to hear from us. He truly wants a close relationship with us. And yes, we truly can have a close relationship with the Lord. We can talk to him, and he will hear us and answer us, not always the answer we want. But he will answer us with love and always do what's best for us. We must be meek and kind to all people. Not just the ones we like but all people. It's easy to be nice to people we like and that are nice to us, and so much harder to be nice to those who are mean to us. But that is being meek, caring about someone else and their needs. No matter how they've treated us we must show them kindness and God's love. A lot of people are mean to others because they are jealous and want what they have. Sometimes it's because they can see Jesus in you and want to know him but don't know how to come out and talk to you about it, so they are mean and aggressive. I know it's difficult to see through their hardness but there is a tender spot in there somewhere no matter how harsh they act. A lot of times they don't even know what they are feeling and don't understand themselves why they treat you and other Christians the way they do. They just know they want what you have.

We also aren't supposed to be boisterous and loud, not brawlers or gossips but humble and meek. Being loud and trying to bring attention to ourselves is the opposite of being meek. We are to be quiet, to listen and speak softly. The Bible states that the meek shall have peace. Not just a little peace but an abundance of peace. An abundance is a whole lot of peace! *But the meek shall inherit the earth; and shall delight themselves in the abundance of peace, Psalms 37:11.* Peace and meekness are treasures that each of us should seek diligently. The good thing is we don't have to go searching for a map hidden in some old trunk somewhere. All we need to do is open our Bible, and if we don't have one, we should get one, you'd be surprised at the wonderful treasures found in its pages. Many Christians say they are rich. They are not talking about money and possessions. They are talking about the Lord and the beautiful treasures that loving Him and His word bring. The treasure that living a good and peaceful life brings.

To speak evil of no man, to be no brawlers, but gentle, shewing all meekness unto all men, Titus 3:2. Here we see again that we are supposed to be gentle and show meekness to everyone. Everyone, not just a few but everyone. That passage touches my heart to such a great degree.

It reminds me to be gentle and to love everyone and to speak evil of no one. The Bible also speaks about someone smiting you on one cheek to give them the other also. That is true meekness. *Ye have heard that it hath been said, An eye for an eye, and a tooth for a tooth; But I say unto you, That ye resist not evil; but whosoever shall smite thee on thy right cheek, turn to him the other also, Matthew 5: 38-39*

    The Lord will cast the wicked down and lift up the meek. Fighting and being ill-tempered is not how we as meek ladies act. Being argumentative is also not the mirror of meekness. That personality is not showing meekness; it's showing worldly behavior. That's how the world acts. Not how Christian, ladies behave. That's not how the word of God tells us to be. Now let's think for a minute and be honest, how many of us would allow someone to hit us on one cheek and then turn and give them the other one also? It would be very hard and near impossible to do without God. If we went by what our flesh wants, we'd probably hit them back and show them who they're messing with. That we were more than they bargained for, and we'd put them in their place. But that isn't how a Christian woman of God behaves. Only through God and his love are we able to be meek and show true kindness. To let someone do us wrong and still love them. To forgive and pray for them. To turn the other cheek even if in us it's impossible. But remember through God all things are possible. I want to throw in here that being meek and loving others is truly of God and his word. But that doesn't mean that God intends for his ladies to be abused and to continue in the abuse. That's not at all what he's saying. He's saying that if someone wrongs you to love them and pray for them and try to lead them to him. Please, precious ladies, if there is abuse going on don't just allow it. Go to God in prayer and he will help you. He will lead you in love so you will know what to do. Draw close to him and he will draw close to you. I had no intentions when I started this chapter to include anything about abuse, but God must have had other plans. Just know that God loves you and knows where you are. Keep praying!

We as servants of the Lord must be gentle and not harsh. We should be kind, not showing rudeness or judgement. Remember God is the judge not us. We are supposed to teach the truth to those that oppose themselves. Showing them meekness and love. Have we shown meekness? Love? Also, what about our neighbors? Have we told them our testimonies? Can they see that we are true Christian ladies? Do they even know we're Christians? I had a neighbor die alone in his house a few years back. He lived alone and hardly anyone came to see him. He was in his sixties, drank and smoked a lot. He would come over and talk to us. He knew we were Christians, and that we love God. But sometimes as I look back, I wonder if we said enough and if we did enough. I also know we can't make someone live for God. It's a choice that everyone must make for themselves. God won't force anyone to live for him or to love him. God gives each of us free will. He wants us to *choose* him and not be made to love him. How would you feel if you were made to love someone? Would it truly be from your heart? Or to know someone was made to love you. How would that make you feel?

We must tell them about God and his love and forgiveness, but in the end it's their decision whether to listen and give their hearts to God or to keep living for the world. My point is, don't wait until it's too late to feel bad about their soul and wish you had done more. Talk to them now. Be that witness now not later, or never. Now is the time!

Blessed are the meek: for they shall inherit the earth, Matthew 5:5. God says the meek are blessed. Praise the wonderful name of the Lord! May the Lord help each of us to be meek. May we learn from his teachings and let his love guide us. His blessings are always so wonderful! The word also says the meek shall inherit the earth. Maybe the reason souls aren't coming to God is because we're not meek. Or maybe not meek enough. Maybe we struggle with self-centeredness and need more love and humility, either way God's word remains true. He can help us be meek if we truly want to be. He loves to bless us and help us when we want to do right and when we turn to him. His word states, *the meek shall inherit the earth*. He didn't say they *may* he said they *shall*! That's a definite not a maybe.

Let the spirit lead you into all truth and understanding. That we may have sweet smelling fruits in the day of judgment and not rottenness. When we see someone fall let's not gossip and shout it on the mountain top for the whole world to hear. Instead, let's show them meekness and God's love. Kindness and compassion can help a struggling, fallen person get back on their feet. Whatever we do, we must remember to take all things to God in prayer. We don't want any souls lost. *Brethren, if a man be overtaken in a fault, ye which are spiritual, restore such an one in the spirit of meekness; considering thyself, lest thou shall also be tempted, Galatians 6:1.* To be a Christian lady we must have meekness and love for others. Our character must show humility and kindness. We can't back bite and talk evil of others. That's not what Christian ladies do. Let's be quiet and peaceful and take everything to God in prayer.

But thou, O man of God, flee these things; and follow after righteousness, godliness, faith, love, patience, meekness

1 Timothy 6:11

Chapter 4
Only The Humble

First, we're going to start this chapter with the definition of humility. We must know what it means to be able to apply it appropriately. Many people think that humility means the same thing as meekness. But that isn't the case. They are very different words with very different meanings. Meekness is often associated with gentleness and a calm, quiet demeanor. It involves being patient, teachable and long-suffering, and not easy to anger. A meek person is willing to endure hardships without resentment or retaliation. They have self-control and are peaceful. While humility on the other hand, is about recognizing that we're not superior or above anyone else. Being humble isn't about being stern or walking high and mighty (proud). A humble Christian lady always puts others first. And has compassion for the less fortunate and the hurting souls needing a soft word. A humble person knows their dependence on God and treats others with respect and love. They are willing to serve and put others' needs before their own.

As we can see, they are different words and are applied separately. Now that we know the difference between the two let's dig deeper into humility and being humble. Pride is a big characteristic these days. With all the selfies and *all about me* attitudes. Do we realize that those thoughts and actions are totally against Gods word. They are not humility, the total opposite. They are pride plain and simple. God's word says, *Pride goeth before destruction, and an haughty spirit before a fall, Proverbs 16:18.* Maybe that's why we must be shaken out of our routine, to put humility back in our hearts. There are consequences of a prideful spirit, they lead to downfall and ruin. Many people have walked away from the teachings of the Bible about humility and being humble. But it's in the Lord's teachings none the less.

If my people which are called by my name, shall humble themselves, and pray, and seek my face, and turn from their wicked ways; then will I hear from heaven, and will forgive their sin, and will heal their land, II Chronicles 7:14. The Lord wants his people to turn away from their wickedness. Not just turn a little, but to turn from it completely. We can't live wickedly and do our own thing and expect to be right with God. That's not what the word of God says. We should shun all ungodliness and turn our faces toward God. We must lay pride and arrogance down at Jesus feet. We need to put down all evil and live holy, peaceful, modest lives. We must always seek to be modest ladies, and humility is part of being truly modest.

We can't do as the world does. We must pray and do as the Lord teaches. God called us out to be a separate people and not follow worldly ways. Instead, he showed us to be different from the world around us. They must see God in us. And if we look and do as the world does all they will see is the world not God. We must be different on the inside and the outside. We can't just display modesty and humility on the outside. We must be modest and humble on the inside first. Trust me, however, your soul is on the inside will show on the outside for everyone to see. We want to be true beacons of love, modesty and humility. Not for our glory but for the glory of God! We should all want and desire to be right on the inside, and for our heart to be right with God. We must shine for him, like a beacon, for all to see! When people look at us, they should see holiness and a spirit of humility. *Whosoever shall humble himself as this little child, the same is greatest in the kingdom of heaven, Matthew 18:4.*

We should humble ourselves as little children. Trust God and know that he has our best interest at heart. If you want to be great in God's eyes, humble yourself as a child. Believe as a child would, with no doubts, just trust. If he says it, know it to be truth. He is our father; he loves us and wants us to trust him. We must know he will lead us in the way we should go, even in our darkest time. No, we cannot become a child again, but we can have a humble spirit as a child. A child trusts its parents and does what they say, they do as they're told because they know their parents wouldn't tell them to do anything that would hurt them. They have total trust. God wants the same thing from us, total trust. He is our father; we should trust him and do what his word tells us to do. No grumbling, talking back or obeying him in the wrong attitude. Rather say yes with a humble heart ready and willing to do his perfect will. He loves us like no person ever could. He knows the beginning from the end. His will not ours.

And when he was in affliction, he besought the Lord his God, and humbled himself greatly before the God of his fathers, II Chronicles 33:12.
I know it is hard to go through life's challenges

but sometimes it takes affliction for us to humble ourselves as we should. Often God will break our routine to strengthen us and our faith in him. Trust me, I know it's hard to go through bad times. We all go through them, and none of us like them because of the flesh. Many of us don't like change at all. We like things to continue to go smoothly. But sometimes God has to shake us up and bring us out of our routine to strengthen us and prepare us for his will. Think of Job and all he went through, but he continued to pray and love God. He went through persecutions and disease that a lot of us would not survive. The Lord wants a close relationship with us, not just a casual acquaintance. He doesn't want to be a fair-weather friend. Just a mere friendship isn't enough. He wants his people to love him from deep within their heart and soul. He wants true humility and love, for us to be real and not play games. Salvation is not to be taken lightly. It is very serious, and if not taken seriously we could get burned.

Better is it to be of an humble spirit with the

lowly, than divide the spoil with the proud, Proverbs 16:19. This verse truly touches the heart. How many of us have listened to other people and done things that in our heart we knew we shouldn't do. But we did it anyway because of their influence and we ended up getting in trouble. We were led by worldly pride and not by Gods word. Most of the time we're the ones that pay for what we did and not the person that talked us into it! We think they get off scot-free, but trust me, sooner or later everyone pays for their wrongs. The Lord expects us to love everybody and to do good to all people. But he does not expect you to hang around evil people or people that always get you in trouble and tell you to do wrong! *Wherefore come out from among them, and be ye separate, saith the Lord, and touch not the unclean thing; and I will receive you, II Corinthians 6:17.* The word says it plainly. Come out from among them and be separate. That's plain, he doesn't say hang out with them or go to their houses and party with them (which Christian ladies would never do!). He also says

not to touch the unclean thing (so that takes care of partying and doing all those sinful things).
But he giveth more grace. Wherefore he saith, God resisteth the proud, but giveth grace unto the humble, James 4:6. We must humble ourselves and pray always. We can't be proud and flaunt our attributes. We don't want the Lord to resist us. We're not supposed to toot our own horns (so to speak). We don't say how wonderful we are as we put others down and magnify their faults. That is not being humble, the total opposite. Please, Ladies don't fall into that trap. And trust me it is a trap that satan uses regularly. If he can get you thinking too highly of yourself then you don't have your mind on the Lord. We must keep our minds on God. We must pray continuously and talk to God always. We don't have to always verbally pray; God can hear us pray even in our thoughts. We can be in the spirit of prayer all day long. *Ephesians 6:18 states, Praying always with all prayer and supplication in the Spirit, and watching thereunto with all perseverance and supplication...*

As we can see throughout this chapter humility and prayer are very important. We must have both to be a true lady of God. We as ladies have a very important role. We are an example to this world of how true Christian woman behave and look. We don't act like everybody else. Look around, do you see Christian ladies at every turn? No, we don't. A true Christian lady is hard to find. We're like a needle in a haystack. If you truly search you can find us, but we are very few. The Lord intends all of us to have those qualities. The Lord wants us to be holy, Christian ladies that will show his love and compassion with a humble heart. I know that worldly women are far from what the Bible teaches ladies to be, but we're not supposed to be following them. We are to follow the Lord and his teachings for us. Remember, we must have humility in the heart and mind. We'd rather be right with God than to be cool and right with the world. The world is lost. We have the road map with the directions on how to be right with God and how to one day be with him in his kingdom. The humble are God seekers. They don't seek to look like the world. They seek God and His word above all else; material things are not in the forefront of their thoughts. Don't misunderstand, God loves to bless us, but we must seek him first in all things. That's what he asks, to love him more than anything else. *But seek ye first the kingdom of God, and his righteousness; and all these things shall be added unto you, Matthew 6:33*

And whosoever shall exalt himself shall be abased; and he that shall humble himself shall be exalted.

Matthew 23:12

Chapter 5
True Love Conquers

I realize we have touched on love in some of the other chapters, but love is mentioned several times throughout the Bible and is very important to our Christian Walk. Love is a beautiful word, and we hear it all the time. We say it without even thinking many times. But do we really mean it when we say it or are we just saying it? Do others mean it when they say it to us? Do any of us know what true love is? We do know true love is hard to find. We've all heard that saying. But tell me, how many of us want to be in love and want to be loved in return? It's our human nature. We want to find that one true love, someone who will love us no matter what. With a true, selfless love. That sees our faults and loves us anyway. God instilled that need in us. And let me tell you, if you know Jesus then you know true love. God is love and he truly loves each of us. He has a deeper love for us than we can ever imagine. Jesus loved us more than life! Think about it, he died and gave up his life for us, so that we might be saved. There is no truer love than that. He knows each of us individually and loves us through our faults. He loves us even though he knows we sin and have a sinful nature. He hates the sin but loves the sinner. Does he want us to sin? No, he doesn't. He wants us to strive for perfection in him. We're his children, he made us and molded us. He wants us to love others as he loves us. God also says in his word that we are to love our neighbor as ourselves. Do we? To do this we must ask the question, *who is our neighbor*? The Bible isn't talking about just your neighbors that live next to you. Jesus is talking about loving all others. God is love and we are to love the way he does. *...That ye love one another; as I have loved you, that ye also love one another. By this shall all men know that ye are my disciples, if ye have love one to another, John 13:34.* Do we truly have that kind of love? Or do we pretend to? We can't pretend to love, Jesus knows the difference. He knows our heart and our thought's. And believe it or not others know if you truly love them and if you truly care. They can tell by your actions and your words. Let's go further, do we love the Lord the way we're supposed to? Or have we said it for so long that it's just habit? Do we love him with our whole heart, or do we just give him part of us? We're supposed to love him with our whole heart. We must give him all that is within us. Jesus doesn't ask for part of us, he wants all of us. We can't just pray and read his word every now and then and expect to love him and live for him with our whole heart. Ladies, let's be honest, if we just talked to our husband every now and then would we have a good relationship with him? Would we truly love him? Is that how we show love? No, it isn't. Communication is very important to every relationship. A relationship dies without communication. We don't want our relationship with our husband to wither away to nothing. So, if we wouldn't act that way with our spouse (or at least I hope not), why would we dare to act that way with our Lord and Savior? We definitely don't want our relationship with him to be distant and to die from lack of communication and prayer. When Jesus says love him with our whole heart that's what he means. All of us. Our heart, our mind and everything within us. We are to give our all to him.

We are also to love one another as Jesus has loved us. Wow! That's a lot of love! We've discussed how much he truly loves us. He lived and died for us because he loves us so much. He hung on the cross with nails driven through his hands and feet. He went through excruciating pain for us and our souls. And in the end, as he was dying, he didn't cry out for himself but for everyone, including the sodier's, the Jewish leaders, and all humanity. He thought of us not himself. He spoke those words for every sinner.

He said, *Father, forgive them for they know not what they do...* Luke 23:34. That's love at its finest and most intense. He said forgive them even though they drove nails through his hands and feet. Even though they beat him and crucified him. That's true love! Could we do that? Can we love so much that we would forgive as we are being tortured and criticized? Are we at that point? The point where no matter what is done to us or said about us, we forgive? There is no stronger love than the Lord's love for us. I pray that the Lord touches us and gives us love overflowing so we may have compassion for others and not think only of ourselves. Thinking only of self is not what the Bible teaches. We must think of others and their needs first. God never said not to love yourself, He said love others first. May Gods love spill over to everyone that encounters us. Whether it be in the grocery store or shopping, wherever we go. And may we care enough to call and check up on those who are sick or homebound. May we somehow help them, comfort them, and talk to them about our wonderful Savior. He wants everyone to come to him. We must have love and compassion for the lost souls that the Lord puts before us. We also must not scare them away with rudeness, pride and self-centeredness. *Love ye therefore the stranger: for ye were strangers in the Land of Egypt, Deuteronomy 10:19.* We are to love even strangers, people we don't know. We don't have to know someone to love them with God's love. If we can't love those whom we don't know and have seen, how can we love God whom we haven't seen?

But Whoso hath this world's good, and seeth his brother have need, and shutteth up his bowels of compassion from him, how dwelleth the love of God in him? My little children, let us not love in word, neither in tongue; but in deed and in truth, I John 3:17-18. Did you feel that nudge? that tinge in the pit of your stomach? I know I did! That really hits the heart! How many times have we seen someone in need and did nothing about it? If they are hungry, we are supposed to feed them. If they are thirsty, we are to give them a drink. We can't just say I hope you find what you need. We are supposed to stop and help them. What are our hearts and eyes set on? Is it on God or this world? *Love not the world, neither the things that are in the world. If any man love the world, the love of the Father is not in him, 1 John 2:15.* Do we walk after the spirit or the flesh? We should walk after the spirit and hate the things even spotted by the flesh. God is love and we must show love from the heart and by our deeds.

For this is the love of God, that we keep his commandments: and his commandments are not grievous, I John 5:3. Let's keep his commandments and love willingly with a pure heart, not with a hardened one. We want to be true Christian ladies not just look like we are on the outside. Remember, being modest starts on the inside. Let's love each other because we love the Lord, and we want to do what he wants us to do. Let not his commandments be grievous but let them bring joy to our heart and to everyone we meet. Living for the Lord and loving the way we should brings joy unspeakable and full of glory!

Let's try it and see how wonderful it is to love and to help others. Open your heart and let others in. It may be hard at first but the more you do it the easier it will become. There are so many ways to help others. We can volunteer at a nursing home or hospital. And maybe even read to the patients. Or maybe help the homeless in a soup kitchen. Volunteer to clean an elderly person's house. Maybe drive an elderly neighbor to their doctor's appointment. If you think about it, you can come up with many ways to help others. It doesn't have to be big things. You can also do small things; God sees everything we do for others and blesses us. Remember to pray and God will lead you to people that need your help. Keep pushing, praying and becoming true Christian ladies in tune to other's needs. Let's love with all our heart and show God's love with our actions and words. We don't have to go alone if we don't want to, grab a friend! I promise you will both be blessed. And remember ladies, God is always with us. May we go together with the power of love to make a difference in the lives of others and the world we live in!

Beloved, let us love one another: for love is of God; and every one that loveth is born of God, and knoweth God. He that loveth not knoweth not God; for God is love.

1 John 4:7-8

Chapter 6
As He Forgives

Forgiveness is so important in our journey to becoming modest, Christian ladies. Forgiving isn't holding grudges and trying to hide every time we see the person that hurt us. We can't hold on to past wrongs and expect to be right with God. I know that sometimes it's hard to forgive, trust me, I really do know. I totally get it; we're all human and tend to want to stay mad. We all go through painful things in our life. It's hard to forgive when someone does us wrong. I'm not about to say it's not. And if I say that I haven't been through things that made me not want to forgive, it wouldn't be true. But we're going to be honest with each other. This book is about us talking as friends and being honest. Not holding back anything or judging one another. We're not here to judge but to lift each other up and to love one another as God loves us. Now let's read the next scripture so we can understand more clearly, *And when ye stand praying, forgive, if ye have aught against any: that your Father also which is in heaven may forgive you your trespasses. But if ye do not forgive, neither will your Father which is in heaven forgive your trespasses, Mark 11:25-26*. And there we have it. The Lord let us know beyond a shadow of a doubt that if we don't forgive then we won't be forgiven. No, it's not easy but we must do it just the same. If someone hurts us and we don't forgive, we start putting our defenses up. We try to keep from getting hurt again so we withdraw ourselves from people. We stop trusting people. When we do this, we build a wall that turns into an iceberg. Seriously, our heart gets cold, and in all actuality, we get lonely and bitter. Please, ladies, don't let this happen to your heart. I assure you, it's not worth it. Don't dwell on it. Pray about it, give it to God, and let it go. More than likely, they have already forgotten what they did, so it's hurting you not them. And if they haven't forgotten they probably just don't care, and it still isn't hurting or bothering them. So don't continue to think about it just give it to God and forget it. Remember, we must forgive them no matter what they do to us. We must love them with Christ like love. We can't control what they do, just what we do and how we respond to their actions. It seems so often that the ones that hurt us the most are the ones that we love and trust the most. There's nothing like thinking you know someone, and you do everything you're supposed to do just to find out they aren't committed to the relationship. That hurts, it's very painful because you trusted that person. But we still must forgive them. We must forgive them like God has forgiven us. No hate, no strife, no wanting to get even. But truly forgive them. I want to add here that forgiveness does not mean you let someone continue to hurt you. Or that you let someone continue to abuse you or run over you. God loves you, he doesn't want that for you. That is not what forgiveness means. It means forgive them and let all the bitterness leave your heart. Pray for them and pray they find Jesus. And friend, give them to God. He will handle it. He knows what it will take to change that person. We can't see into their heart, but God can. I can assure you he knows just how to handle them in his way. He knows what it will take for them to turn from their wicked ways. Trust him!

For us to forgive the way Jesus forgives we must pray and read his word. He died on the cross for us, and them. We didn't deserve forgiveness, we deserved to die for our sins, to burn in the blazing lake of fire. But Jesus, through his wonderful mercy and saving grace took our place. He forgave us for all the sins we've ever committed. If we turn our backs on the transgressions and ask for forgiveness Jesus forgives us. We want to be true Christian ladies. We want to be examples of good women doing our best to live for Jesus. Holding grudges is not modest or Christian. *And be ye kind one to another; tenderhearted, forgiving one another, even as God for Christ's sake hath forgiven you, Ephesians 4:32.*

If we cry out to God and repent with a sincere brokenness, we are forgiven that very moment. After we repent, we must leave those sins at Jesus feet and walk away from them and do our best to do right. Don't keep going back to those things that you gave to Jesus. The past is over and forgiven. Now forgive yourself and give it all to Jesus. He wants to take it. He wants to lift that burden from you. Move forward and no longer dwell on it.

Many people ask the question; *how many times am I supposed to forgive them?* Or they say, *I'll forgive them this time, but they better not do it again because my forgiveness only goes so far.* We can't think like that. I'm so glad Jesus didn't think like that with us. We've all sinned way more than one time and if we were sorry and truly repented God forgave us instantly. We must do the same. We can't limit how many times we forgive. There should be no number and we should not keep a tally of it. Forgiveness should be ongoing and continuous. *Take heed to yourselves: if thy brother trespass against thee, rebuke him; and if he repent, forgive him. And if he trespass against thee seven times in a day, and seven times in a day turn again to thee, saying, I repent; thou shalt forgive him, Luke 17: 3-4.* Many times, people do us wrong over and over and we kick ourselves for letting them get close enough to do it to us again. And it hurts over and over. But if they repent, we still must find it in our heart to forgive them. No, it won't be easy. Yes, we'll have to hit our knees and cry out to God for help. But we must forgive them. We want them to come to Jesus. Ladies, we can do it. Let's pray for each other and lift each other up in our time of need. Let's not be jealous of each other but instead let's be there for one another.

Anger and jealousy are two very destroying emotions. Be very careful with them. They can both destroy our walk with God. We all get angry, it's a normal human emotion but as soon as we feel it, we must deal with it. We can't let it fester in our heart and mind. Anger can make us say and do many things that we truly didn't mean. In anger people burst out words they never would have said had they not been angry. As I mentioned in a previous chapter, once something is said it can't be taken back. It's out there, and no matter how many times we say we're sorry it doesn't change the words that have been said. Sometimes when we're mad, we lash out trying to hurt the person that hurt us, but we can't do that. We must check ourselves when we get angry so we don't say things we will regret later. Modest, Christian ladies can't be angry and hateful all the time. We all have the emotion of anger but when we feel it, we must pray for the strength to push it aside. Remember, if we don't forgive, and truly forgive, Gods word says we won't be forgiven. It's that simple. If his word says it, then it's true.

Rejoice not when thine enemy falleth and let not thine heart be glad when he stumbleth,

Proverbs 24:17. Snickering and being happy because someone falls is not forgiveness. If every time you see the person that wronged you, you have an urge to roll your eyes and stick up your nose, then you haven't truly forgiven that person. Same goes from getting pleasure from their hardships. Forgiveness is laying aside all thoughts of revenge and not wanting anything bad to happen to them. We want everyone to come to God and get right with him. We want them to also have the wonderful joy that Jesus' love and forgiveness brings. We need to pray earnestly for them with a pure heart. May we truly search our heart and humble ourselves before the Lord. May the Lord give us the love and compassion to truly forgive.

"Forbearing one another, and forgiving one another, if any man have a quarrel against any: even as Christ forgave you, so also do ye."

Colossians 3:13

Chapter 7
Necessity Of Faith

Can you imagine a mountain moving just by speaking it in Jesus's name? To see a mountain floating in the sea would be a wonderful, miraculous thing. And all because you spoke it in faith! Do you believe it's possible? Do you believe in miracles? With God all things are possible. I choose to believe God's word and to know in faith that if he said it, he can do it! Read what he says about it, *And Jesus answering saith unto them,*

Have faith in God. For verily I say unto you, That whosoever shall say unto this mountain, Be thou removed, and be thou cast into the sea; and shall not doubt in his heart, but shall believe that those things which he saith shall come to pass; he shall have whatsoever he saith, Mark 11:22-23. That scripture tells me that by believing and having faith all things are possible. Have you ever been down on your luck and desperate? Have you ever cried so hard that all you wanted was to touch God? Have you ever wanted something so bad that you were willing to do anything to get it? Have you ever done without and sacrificed to get it? Have you ever trusted God in faith to receive your blessing? There was a woman in the Bible that trusted Jesus so much that she knew if she could just reach him and touch him that she would be healed. Read about this incident, *And behold, a woman, which was diseased with an issue of blood twelve years, came behind him, and touched the hem of his garment: For she said within herself, If I may but touch his garment, I shall be whole. But Jesus turned him about, and when he saw her, he said, Daughter, be of good comfort; thy faith hath made thee whole. And the woman was made whole from that hour, Matthew 9:20-22.* For twelve years this woman had her issue. That's a long time to suffer. That's a long time to cry and hurt. No person could heal her. She was desperate. She was tired of suffering day in and day out. She only knew one person that could help her. If she could just get to him, if she could just touch him. There were flocks of people standing around, but she pushed through the crowd in anguish, not seeing or hearing their conversations. Their noise was muted because of her desperation and focus to get to Jesus. She heard about the miraculous healings he performed on many before her. She knew he could do the same for her! She found Jesus and came behind him and touched his garment. She just had to touch him, just to feel the hem of his garment in her hand. She was crying, she was desperate. She had to touch Jesus because he was her only hope. She put all her faith into knowing that he would heal her if she could just reach him.

She didn't say she had to talk to him; she just had to touch him. By faith she was made whole that very moment! Not an hour or day later, but at that very moment! It wasn't touching Jesus's robe that made her whole it was her faith in knowing that if she could just get to him and reach him that she would be healed. She believed with an unwavering faith. What no physician could do, Jesus did that very hour! Praise the Lord!

I know as humans we go through a lot of things, from emotional, financial, to physical and beyond. We all have difficulties. We all need Jesus. He is the only one that can truly help us. We just need to trust and believe that he has our best interest at heart. Are you desperate? Have you tried everything, and nothing is working? Please, go to Jesus in prayer and have faith knowing he will hear you and bless you. Here is another scripture about faith and believing about two blind men, *And when Jesus departed thence, two blind men followed him, crying and saying, Thou son of David have mercy on us. And when he was come into the house, the blind men came to him: and*

Jesus saith unto them, Believe ye that I am able to do this? They said unto him, Yea, Lord. Then touched he their eyes, saying, According to your faith be it unto you, Matthew 9:27-29. He just asked the blind men if they believed he was able to do this? He wanted to hear them confess their faith. Did they believe? Yes, they believed and according to their faith it was done unto them. Their faith was unwavering. They were blind but they still believed that Jesus would heal them, and he did! They had faith before they even saw the miracle. A lot of people only believe something if they see it. But God is asking us to believe without seeing, to have faith and know that his word is true. We must believe that what we ask and pray for, Jesus will do, in his way and in his time. We must believe in our heart and mind that nothing is too hard for God. God's word is true and what his word says, he will do. Eyes are opened and diseases are healed. Nothing is too hard for him.

  I gave a couple examples in this chapter but there are many more. What a wonderful God we serve! Praise his holy name! Could you imagine the wonderful things that could happen in our cities, state and country if we prayed and believed. What changes could be made by praying? The bad that could be turned into good by having faith that God will do it. By having faith without seeing the miracle but knowing in our heart and mind that it's going to happen? Why? Because Jesus said It! We can't believe a lot of what people tell us or what they say, but we can believe Gods word every time!

Will Jesus find faith when he returns? Will we be praying instead of complaining about things happening to us or in our world today? Prayer changes things. It truly does! Believe me, prayer works. I've had many answered prayers and miracles in my life. If he'll do it for me, he will do it for you. You must have faith believing he can do it. Do I have something you don't have? No, I don't, I just have faith!

Are our hearts and eyes on this world and on the flesh? Not having enough faith could be the reason our many infirmities are not healed. Jesus says, *have faith*. If we have faith, he will do the rest. Don't let the world put disbelief in your mind and don't let satan either. The devil will do his best to make you doubt. Doubt is the opposite of faith. We must humble ourselves and pray always. If we have a problem, we should always bring it to God in prayer. We can't handle our problems and burdens, but Jesus can! *And the prayer of faith shall save the sick, and the Lord shall raise him up; and if he have committed sins, they shall be forgiven him, James 5:15.*

How do we get this kind of faith? By reading our Bible and praying. Reading the Bible is an absolute necessity. How can we know what it says if we don't read it? And we must pray with sincerity. Sometimes life is so hard, we all know it's true, but with Jesus the load is lighter. He walks with us and if we listen closely with our heart, he talks to us. Let's take on the shield of faith so we can quench every dart and attack from the enemy and all his demons. Let's have the kind of faith that moves mountains and see what kind of miracles God works on our behalf! Faith is very powerful! He will show each of us women how to be faithful ladies for him. Just ask him. Give all your burdens to him, sit back, have faith, and see what blessings and wonders he sends your way.

"For we walk by faith, not by sight."

2 Corinthians 5:7

Chapter 8
Dedication To Prayer And Worship

My voice shalt thou hear in the morning, O Lord; in the morning will I direct my prayer unto thee, and will look up, Psalms 5:3. We should always start our day with prayer and worship. Prayer helps the day get started right. God wants us to pray and talk to him always. You'd be surprised how much better your day would be if you started every morning off this way. Starting our day in prayer will get us in tune with the Lord and help us to put the flesh aside and walk after the things of the spirit. We must die daily to this flesh. Prayer always starts the day out right! We should pray to God continuously in our hearts. I know we can't pray verbally all day long because we must go through our daily life. But we can have a prayer in our heart continuously. We are not able to physically pray all day, but we can be in the spirit of prayer all day. We don't have to be on our knees to pray. I pray in my car or wherever I am. Yes, you can pray with your eyes open. God hears whenever and however you pray. Praise and prayer are very important to our walk with the Lord. He likes to hear from us. We are his children. What parent doesn't enjoy hearing from their children? Our prayers are the Lord's delight! He loves for us to talk and communicate with him. The more we pray the more sensitive we become to God's will and to his voice. God does talk to each of us; we just have to listen with ears willing to hear what he has to say. God loves us and wants a relationship with us, but we must be willing to pray. He never leaves us alone. So, when you feel alone just remember God is there with you. He hears and answers prayer. It may not be when we want him to or exactly the way we ask, but God knows best. He always does everything for our good. He always hears when we cry out to him. We are never too far or too deep in sin, he still hears us and loves us. He wants to bless us and fill our lives and hearts with joy.

He even hears people in prison. *Peter therefore was kept in prison: but prayer was made without ceasing of the church unto God for him. And when Herod would have brought him forth, the same night Peter was sleeping between two soldiers, bound with two chains: and the keepers before the door kept the prison. And behold, the angel of the Lord came upon him, and a light shined in the prison: and he smote Peter on the side, and raised him up, saying, Arise up quickly. And his chains fell off from his hands, Acts 12: 5-7.* This scripture is a wonderful example of the answer to prayer. The church prayed without ceasing on Peter's behalf. They didn't stop nor did they give up! They kept praying until they touched

God for him. There were guards on either side of Peter but that didn't stop God. He was bound with chains, but that didn't stop God either! He sent an angel and those chains fell off. The Lord is mighty and so worthy to be praised. He's mightier than any problem we may have. No matter if we are bound with physical chains or emotional ones the Lord can deliver us from every stronghold. Nothing is too big or too hard for him. Prayer can do mighty things. Things we can't even imagine. *And all things, whatsoever ye shall ask in prayer, believing, ye shall receive, Matthew 21:22.*

God knows our needs, but he likes to hear from us. He doesn't work on a time clock, instead he is always there when we call his name. No matter what we're going through he is with us. And even when we are tempted, he has us covered. This scripture plainly states, *and when he rose up from prayer, and was come to his disciples, he found them sleeping for sorrow, And said unto them, why sleep ye? Rise and pray, lest ye enter into temptation, Luke 22:45-46.* Satan will try to tempt us every time he has the chance. He will put obstacles in our way and try to keep us from doing things we know we have to do, like for instance prayer and worship. We must be prayed up! We must go boldly to the throne of God and lay all our cares at his feet. Not arrogantly, but in love and humility. How will we know how to be modest, Christian ladies for him if we don't talk to him? God will give us direction if we just ask. I know sometimes we can pray, and it seems like nothing is happening. Just remember God also works in the background and you may not see what he's doing but he is working everything out for your good. Trust me, God cares, and he hears. He will light your pathway; you just have to be willing to walk where he illuminates.

Pray and worship the Lord while you're waiting for his wonderful will and direction. Jesus loves his children to worship him, its music to his ears. *But the hour cometh, and now is, when the true worshippers shall worship the Father in spirit and in truth: for the Father seeketh such to worship him, John 4:23.* We must worship the Lord in spirit and in truth. Why? Because he is worthy of all praise and we love him. Sing praises to his holy name! *For thou shalt worship no other god: for the LORD, whose name is Jealous, is a jealous God, Exodus 34:14.* God is a jealous God. Have no other gods before him. He is the only God worthy of praise and worship. Some people make things of this world their gods. They worship movie stars and worldly possessions. We must not do that. That hurts Jesus and is against his word and will. He is a jealous God and will not tolerate it. He won't be second to anything or anyone! He should always be first in our lives. I want Jesus to forever be first in my life. He's my father and I love him with all that is within me. He gave up his life for us because he loves us. He didn't have to do it, but he did it because he truly loves his children. He wants our love and dedication back. He wants our lives to show his love. We must show others what wonderful things God has done for us. We must share his love with them, let them know he died for them and their sins. There is no other love greater than this. His heart hurts when he sees vindictiveness and meanness. Ladies let's never show anything but kindness and love to everyone. May others come to God by our words and actions. Remember to Praise and worship the Lord for he is so worthy!

"Make a joyful noise unto the LORD, all the earth: make a loud noise, and rejoice, and sing praise."

Psalms 98:4

Chapter 9
True Holiness

Give unto the Lord the glory due unto his name: bring an offering and come before him; worship the Lord in the beauty of holiness, I Chronicles 16:29. What is Jesus talking about in this scripture? I want to be holy and right with God. Holiness is beautiful to the Lord. God expects His women to be holy. But again, what does that mean? I have searched the word holiness in the dictionary. Holiness means purity of heart or dispositions; sanctified affections; piety; moral goodness. That which is separated to the service of God. Now we know what it means, but how do we apply it to our life?

Holiness is an absolute necessity for a child of God. Holiness is very important in our walk with him. We must be different than the world, inside and out. A true Christian lady looks and acts different from the world. We must worship the Lord in the beauty of holiness. We aren't supposed to try to look gaudy and made up. That's not what makes us beautiful to God. He wants inner beauty with outward manifestation that shows the world we live for him. We can't just act and look any way we want and expect to be holy. We are rare, not part of the world around us that lust after things of the flesh. There aren't many holy women out there. Look around and you will see very worldly women that aren't feminine or holy. It's not just what we look like on the outside, but holiness comes from the inside and shines through to the outside. When we meet others, they should feel holiness through our pure conversations. Not better than thou attitude but a true personality of love and compassion for others. We want others to see Jesus in us through our speech and our appearance. We want everyone to know Jesus. He's the healer, the prince of peace and our comforter. He's the alpha and omega, the beginning and the end. He's the only hope for a lost and dying world. They must see holiness in us. We must be meek and humble. We need to stand strong in the truth and do what is right no matter what others are doing. Remember, we want to be modest, Christian ladies. *Follow peace with all men, and holiness, without which no man shall see the Lord, Hebrews 12:14.* That scripture tells us very plain that if we do not have holiness, we will not see the Lord. We ladies show holiness in many ways, through how we speak, act, and even through what we wear and choose not to wear. People look at us and see something different, they don't know exactly what it is, but they want it. They can't put their finger on it, but they know it's right. They can feel God in us.

Christian women stand out from the crowd, not join it. We're not necessarily trying to stick out.

We're not trying to get noticed because of our works but because God is in us and we are doing what the Bible says. It's the decision we made to be holy and live in truth that makes us different. Rejoice In your difference and be glad you made the choice to turn your back on worldly ways. And that you turned toward God and his ways. Jesus is so wonderful! He shows each of us individually what he wants for us and for our lives. Listen to that small faint voice and he will lead you to all understanding.

If you truly want to know truth and how to be holy, God will show you how. There are many ways to show holiness. Like for instance, being submissive to our husbands. I felt someone cringe when they read those words. But ladies it is Biblical. I do want to make something clear though, so you don't get the wrong idea of what being submissive means. It does not mean walking ten feet behind your husband nor bowing down to them and their every whim. We are their helpmeet, not their door mat to wipe their feet on. We are ladies and expect to be treated as such.

Don't expect or accept anything less. We are to be wise in our conversations with our husbands. Not put them down all the time but see their good qualities and lift them up in love. We are to be one in God. Work together, love one another and be true to each other. *"Likewise, ye wives, be in subjection to your own husbands; that, if any obey not the word, they also may without the word be won by the conversation of the wives, I Peter 3:1.*" The unsaved husbands should be able to look at us and our conversations and see holiness. They could come to God by our words and actions.

Being loud and boisterous is not how a submissive lady behaves. That's how worldly women in bars and clubs behave. That is far from meekness and holiness. We should be meek with a quiet spirit, and not loud and argumentative. Holiness is not just an outward appearance but also an inward experience. Once you experience it you won't want to go back to the lost world's ways. When you are holy and clean on the inside it will show on the outside. Don't fret, pray and let God lead you. Remember, it is God in us that makes us holy. He will lead us and guide us into holiness if we just ask him. He wants to show us his ways; he just wants us to pray and ask for his guidance. We must be an example of truth and holiness. Its Gods will, his word and what he desires of us. Not with a heavy heart but with love for him. His ways are not cumbersome when we love him and want to do his will. Let's cloak ourselves with holiness and show the world that it's possible to be true women of God! We must follow and obey his example of true holiness. If we have questions about holiness, we can take them to God in prayer, and he will answer us and show us what we need to know.

Holiness is falling by the wayside. Women have set aside holiness to be worldly and have the worlds sins. Many are following the lust of the eyes and body and not giving thought to the consequences of such actions. They use ungodly women as examples of what they think is right. But ladies it's not right. We can't follow them to destruction; we must follow Jesus to righteousness and holiness. Satan is trying to get us women to follow him because of vanity and sin. We can't look at what others do, we must look to Jesus and his principles and scriptures of what is right. Don't fall for satan's lies! Remember, he will deceive you if you let him. Don't let him lead you away from God and his ways. *"Be sober be vigilant; because your adversary the devil, as a roaring lion, walketh about, seeking whom he may devour." 1Peter 5:8.*

Toss vanity aside and stand strong in holiness the way God intends his ladies to be! Be the example of holiness and sobriety. Stand firm in the faith and don't waver. Don't watch the world and what they are doing. Show the world God in you. Don't look to the left or to the right but keep your eyes focused on Jesus and his kingdom. Live holiness in all joy and consecration, because you are a child of the king! And one glorious day we will be with him in is kingdom!

"For God hath not called us unto uncleanness, but unto holiness."

1 Thessalonians 4:7

Chapter 10
Our Outer Appearance

Okay, ladies, we've discussed our inward qualities of how to be modest, Christian ladies. Now we must talk about our outer appearance. I know a lot of you may be saying, *here we go, I knew she would try to tell us how to dress.* But you will be happy to know, I'm not. I'm going to use God's word and scriptures to show what we should do. It's not my opinion but God's word that counts so that's what we're going by.

We want God's will not our will, definitely not

my will, but his will. There are wonderful qualities that others notice just by looking at us. The saying, *first impressions are lasting impressions,* is a true statement. How many times have we met someone and automatically in our mind thought that they were trouble only to find out later that we were right? We didn't get that impression only from their outward appearance. We got that from the way they carried themselves, the way they talked, and the way they acted. But I'm also sure the outward appearance had some bearing on our decision. Sometimes it's just a feeling we get. Our gut instinct. There are many fake people out there and usually a Christian can spot them a mile away. We automatically know we don't want what they have, as a matter of fact we try to stay as far away as possible. The Lord says to, *come out from among them, and be ye separate, II Corinthians 6:17.*

He's not saying be better than thou, haughty or rude. That's not what he wants at all. Ladies, we are examples to the world and to our daughters of how to be Christians. We must show modesty by our appearance, speech and our actions. If they can't see a difference in us, then who? Hollywood with all their sexual exploits of children in pictures and tv? By half-dressed models in magazines. What has happened to women being true feminine, modest ladies? True lovers of Christ and his word? We must obey God's commandments and not look to the world or listen to their sinful lies. If it's against God's truth, then it's a lie. And we want no part of the filth and lies that the world and media try to shove down our throat.

The Lord is coming, and I want to be ready to meet him when he does. This world is in more chaos and filth than I've ever seen it. I refuse to be a part of it. The Bible tells us to be separate from the ways of the world. There must be an outer distinction between Christian women and worldly women. Even Adam and Eve once their eyes were opened sewed fig leaves together and made themselves aprons. *And they heard the voice of the Lord God walking in the cool of the day: and Adam and his wife hid themselves from the presence of the Lord God amongst the trees of the garden, Genesis 3:8.* Why do you think they hid themselves? They had sewn fig leaves for covering. Then why? Because God had opened their eyes and they saw their nakedness was sin. They knew the fig leaves barely covered their nakedness. How did they know they were naked? Why were they ashamed of their nakedness? Because they did what God commanded them not to do, they ate of the tree they weren't supposed to touch. From that moment on they knew they were naked and that their nakedness was a sin. Their eyes were opened. Many people today are blinded by satan's lies and deceit. Many seek the latest fashion, not giving any thought to modesty or decency. They want to be vogue and follow the worldly styles that fashion designers portray. They think people will like the fashions they wear and want to be like them. The world is undressing themselves more and more. It's unbelievable to the extent they've gone. You can't even pick up a paper or magazine without seeing the corruption of the world today. That's why we must be that example. They must be able to see modest, Christian women that live by the Lord's commandments in dress. We can't follow the trends and the styles of this lost world. We must follow God and His word.

Unto Adam also and to his wife did the Lord God make coats of skins, and clothed them, Genesis 3:21. Their clothing of fig leaves were inadequate for covering so God clothed them correctly. God's word is filled with examples of how to behave as well as how to dress. We must adhere to his laws and commandments. We must ask the Lord to show us his will and to open our eyes to his truth. If we ask with a repented heart and a mind wanting to know truth, he will show us the right way to dress. He will light our path, so we choose the right one. He will walk with us and help us if we fall. As humans we will fall but the Lord will always pick us up. He will never give us more than we can handle. I promise you we can do it. We can consecrate our lives to God, his will and his ways. We are not saved by our goodness or by what we wear. I want to make that fact plain. We do these things because we love the Lord, and he tells us to follow his commandments and to be saved by his grace. We are not worthy, we are sinners. But our appearance is an outward dedication to God and to show the world that we love the Lord and abide by his commandments. We are happy to be Christian women. His commandments are not troublesome but are a pure pleasure and a true blessing. I want the Lord to know I love him by my actions and by my dress. We also don't have to be fanatical to please God. We must not think that our clothing will save us because it won't. We aren't dressing modestly to *be* saved we are modest because we *are* saved. Remember, being modest always starts on the inside. Our heart must be right with God. And we get right with the Lord by reading His word and praying. That's why I chose the outward appearance as the last chapter in this book, because you must be right on the inside first. If we're right on the inside, it will shine through to the outside! People will see us and want what we have. They will want to know Jesus too.

I hope this book has shown some wonderful ways to be modest, Christian ladies. I also hope you have gathered up the precious nuggets of truth and placed them in your heart. May we each realize that being modest isn't just about us, but it's also for our daughters and young ladies coming up. They can't look to the world and see Godly principles; they must look to us as examples and look to God's word. Please, ladies realize the huge responsibility we have in rearing and raising our future ladies. It must start with us! Put on the robe of strength, modesty and virtue. Be a leader in what is true and right! And be that mirror reflecting God's marvelous light.

"The woman shall not wear that which pertaineth unto a man, neither shall a man put on a woman's garment: for all that do so are abomination unto the LORD thy God."

Deuteronomy 22:5

www.ingramcontent.com/pod-product-compliance
Lightning Source LLC
LaVergne TN
LVHW051135080426
835510LV00018B/2419